27 Mystical and musing

A prose-like journey with inspiring ditties that will bring on a smile
By Doris Richardson-Edsell
Copyright and photos by Doris Richardson-Edsell March 13, 2015
Dedicated to Joseph R. who inspires me to be musing and hopeful
To Brenda Carol Bradshaw who helped bring about clarity for all of us

Introduction:
Musing

Climb up your playground in musical, playful ways

A friend calls me his muse, and when I thought about it, I guess I am a muse. A muse writes in beautiful, prose-like ways to inspire others, putting a warm smile on many people who need a positive moment. And like music, a muse has a rhythmic way of sending messages to others, and I am hoping that my musical ways can help you on a gray day.

Positive, playful moments

Make every day in your life a pleasant one by changing something about yourself right now that brings out the playfulness in you. Play just for a few moments by stretching, flexing and breathing. These playful moments can start you up for the day.

Pass along your musing ways to others by being powerfully optimistic and positive; helping people to see that putting on a smile can be passed along to others one by one.

1. Ways to be more musing and hopeful

Should you be swinging?

Humming, dancing, writing down some *wonder words* and moving about helps you in so many healing ways. Try some movement first; gracefully stretching to the sky, arms up with feet planted into the ground, and moving about in child-like ways, smiling, giggling and laughing.

Still

Then stay still for a moment, soaking in where you are; allowing your spirit to rise, smiling at you. Your spirit gives you the space to just be in the moment, free of worry, free of sadness and grief; full of joyful, moving and swaying ways.

Music Moves Me

It does not have to be a challenge, just do something musical. And if music helps you find your way to this blissful space in your heart center, turn it up, or keep it soft, whatever it is that brings you here in the moment in healing, energizing ways.

Listening to the sounds of bells

Bells bring on hope, love and balance. Hear the bells in your head, ring bells slowly or quickly; guiding you toward sounds that are different in pitch. And then go outdoors and hear the sounds of the birds softly and loudly singing their tunes in graceful ways. Listen to the music in running water, guiding you to be with the flow of things as water gracefully rides its purposeful path moving the icy ways of winter along to spring. Listen and be still to the sounds of music that rides along in your *mind's eye.* Wondering, creating and soothing moments with you find their ways into others.

 And you become that person who is softer, kinder and more loving.

2. Just One More Joyful Moment

Where are your imbalances in life?

When things hurt, remember that *this too shall pass* and embrace the pain because right around the corner there will be moments of joy. And when that joy surrounds you, do not forget the pain; bring it back in front of you for a closer look so that you know where you are right now in the bliss of life.

Pain is part of living life. If you did not have pain you would not know how good true joy feels. And joy is more than happiness. Joy surrounds you, deep down into your soul; waking things up inside so that you can move with grace; lightly on your toes, reaching up to the sky and feeling grateful that you are here in this moment. Pain hurts but when it is gone, you may forget the pain, and that is good.

Joy is true bliss and when you do not have it, you know it is gone, and because of the chronic longing for happiness and joy, you begin the search; to seek out joy every single day of your life so that you can just have one more moment.

3. Trip but do not fall

Remember the last time you were *tripped up?*

A physical trip is easy to remember such as that jagged rock or that short step that you missed and you caught yourself thinking, "I am so glad I did not fall."

What about the trips in your mind and soul?

Do you trip up by saying something you should not have said? Or do you feel like things are not moving as fast as you would like them to in a relationship so you push, and that push brings on a fall instead of a trip.

Being patient

When you are patient and wait for things to unfold, you will find greater success than when you are pushing things all of the time. In your mind you may think that you need to push sometimes because nothing good seems to happen when you just wait patiently. But like paint drying, you cannot stick your fingers in the paint too early or you will have to start over again with another coat of paint. In the long run, patience truly is a virtue in life's adventures. Today, wait and see what will unfold for you and the ones you love.

4. Stand Tall

It is time to put your shoulders back, bending at the waist which lifts up your abdomen for good breathing, and then tuck your chin in, and looking straight ahead. It is time to show yourself and others how strong you are because you need to stand tall like a tree with strong branches and a straight trunk.

Life Goals

If your goals are material things, get rid of that thought and move on to the things in life that truly matter. This is the time to rid yourself of those material things that stop you from feeling well in mind, body and spirit.

Things

Many things get in your way. Not just those old *nick knacks* that you should rid yourself of but those bad thoughts need consideration too. Bad thinking brings about an attitude of powerlessness and frustration.

Aging brings you a soft sense of life

No more hard times, just softness is my goal today. I want contentment, peacefulness and a powerful sense of love from myself and others. That is all that I need. As you age those things you thought you needed are not in your field of vision. Your vision in life is internal bliss with your spirit guiding you toward helping you with stillness, balance and harmony like a soft wave gently touching your toes as you sit by that stream.

When you bring clarity into your life by removing not just the things you do not use anymore, (that is a good start) but also removing the negative thoughts and behaviors that may be bringing you much sadness and distress. Do not pack things away, hidden from your eyes; give them to someone who may benefit you're your treasures. Begin to remember that the physical treasures that you have collected over the years are just things without meaning.

5. Circles of ancient ways

Circling back to childhood

I remember as a small child being at my grandmother's home. I was always looking around her home because it was so very different. There were many things from Italy that sparkled and left me in awe. Grandma had large pictures of Christ hanging on the wall and rosary beads everywhere because there was always time to pray. Of upmost importance was the ancient craft of crocheting. Grandma, my aunts and mother all knew how to crochet.

Sauce and Garlic

My grandmother's house smelled of garlic. Garlic was used for everything including medicinal ways; stringing it and hanging it around your neck at night could cure just about anything along with keeping away some evil spirits who may be keeping you sick. Every single time I entered grandma's house I not only smelled garlic but there was the deep lovely smell of fresh tomatoes that she was canning and a large pot of sauce on the stove. As I walked by the stove she asked me in her thick soft Italian voice to stir the sauce, and as I did I saw large meat balls inside and an egg still in the shell. Eggs were supposed to take away any bitterness from the sauce.

Of course you had to sprinkle some extra salt into the sauce (throwing any residue behind your left shoulder) and if you were really hungry there may have been some rabbit inside the pot for some added protein which was scary because sometimes the head of the rabbit was still there. But the most significant things in my grandma's house were her doilies. White starched doilies placed neatly under each large lamp that were statues of ancient couples all dressed up in their Sunday best; antiques from Italy with wonderful green and red colors.

Doilies

I did learn how to make those doilies; standing behind mom every single time she picked up a crochet needle, I watched. Today I consider my doilies circles of energy that I know come back to me for healing moments when I need them. I do not starch them but they lie in the center of my dining room table when there is company coming for dinner.

6. Energize yourself and then send it to others on your path

Focus on a circular moment right now where you seem to have gotten to the same place in life. You know that place where you seem to be doing the same things with no results. I always think of relationships and wonder why I end up in the same spot; sometimes good places and sometimes not so good. Like a dog chasing his tail, you may feel that some parts of you are not yours alone. Dogs do not understand that their tail is their own. But you understand everything about yourself including your mind, body and soulful ways. You can begin some positive energy to yourself by centering your focus on those parts that need tending.

Just Breathe

Deep and cleansing breaths with a sound on the exhale can bring new energy into your body. Start your day with your breath; breathing in until your shoulder rise high, holding your breath for a moment, and then breathing out with your new noisy breath, getting all the air out of your body. Do this 3 times upon rising to re-energize yourself for the day.

Self-Discovery, accepting flaws and attitude adjustments

When I dig deep into my inner being, it is not always a pleasant experience. I seem to have many flaws that I have not dealt with very well. I seem to have many lessons to learn about life. Now that I am older I keep thinking that I should have learned just about everything in life that can make my final years better but not all moments are where I want them to be. I remember my mom saying, "It does not matter what happened in the past, it is what you are going to do about yourself right now." And those words are true because stopping or at least slowing down the painful dwelling is the first step toward wellness in any situation. It may be time to stop, focus on the present, the only place where you have control.

Adjustments

You know that everything in life is about your attitude; a positive one can help. You may have a wonderful life full of happy moments and money in your pocket, but if you do not have a special person to share your moments with, you may feel lonely and lost. Or you can have a hard life, filled with more grief than you seem to be able to handle, but your optimism brings you much happiness and contentment.

Today, change your attitude to a more hopeful one and no matter what comes of this moment right now; know that it is perfect; even with all of its flaws. Know that humans are full of flaws, disharmony and imbalances; making it difficult for you to stay focused on the optimistic view of life, but do it anyway. Do it with passion; find the positive between the sadness, loneliness and distractions of living. You will then focus back in harmony. Your circle will become complete with you as the positive and healing energy inside. See yourself with arms raised high pushing the energy from your circle to everyone you see today.

7. What you really need

Do you need to put some playtime into your life?

You may be circling around life moving back toward the same situations but not realizing it because it is with different people. Back and forth you swing. It seems that the inner self comes out to greet you every few years; telling you that we need to change.

Heart Centers

And when your follow that inner heart center; you know the place deep in your soul, things begin to be clear. This clarity allows you to make those needed adjustments in your life but you have to remember that they are not permanent changes. You can start out with good intention and really make some progress in your goals but if you cannot slack off you revert back to your old ways, old habits or old addictions.

It is a constant battle when you start to circle back to the same place. Because life is like a circle of energy, the momentum circles back to you. Sometimes with good new habits that become a part of your spirit, and sometimes bad habits that you did not even notice you were doing over and over again.

What do you really need?

To truly be aware that you have to work on yourself every single day to stay with fresh and positive thoughts that can guide you in a direction that brings about optimism, love, harmony and clarity into your next step.

8.   What do you need to know?

During playtime tap on a drum to bring you clarity

Is it sometimes better to not know the truth about something? I guess in some circumstances, the truth will not *set you free* but most of the time people really need to know the truth, especially about people they may have trusted for many years, or they may have to trust again, or even forgive.

Did you ever suspect someone was not being truthful with you?

And you dismissed it as a fluke; thinking that your insight may have been off a bit, but deep inside you knew that they may have been holding back; perhaps because they did not want to hurt your feelings.

Truth

I would rather know the entire truth about someone because then I can decide whether it is time to move on, or time to forgive the person for not being honest. We all make mistakes and may deserve forgiveness from loved ones when we tell the truth, or may not deserve to be forgiven, but are forgiven anyway. If you lie about something remember that people may never trust you again or they may have to test your strength on truths in the future by you making amends and proving that you can be trusted again.

Respect

You may be respected for *coming clean* on issues that you may be holding inside, and some may understand why you did not tell the truth; with some never understanding.

White Lies

I know from experience that it is better for everyone concerned to hear the truth then it is to be lied to. Sometimes truths have blurred lines; *soft white lies* that may help someone along their path so that they can move on. I am sure you can think of some people who would be better off not knowing details that may hurt them for a very long time. Because of this you may have to keep something from someone until they are old enough or strong enough to hear the truth.

But who is it that gets to decide when the truth will set you free?

9. Bringing you closer

Believe that clarity will come and within it, your life's purpose

Bringing you closer in my life is my focus. I lost track of things for a long moment, but now I know what is important. We all lose track of things that are important and our internal being may be saying, "Put this to the side for now. I am too busy."

What is your primary purpose in life?

To be a loving person to others on your path; that is what we are here for. Do not lose your important focus in life and begin to bring that special person closer to your heart. Whatever it is that you have to do, start now. It may be an extra hug this morning or a pat on the back for a job done well; whatever it is that will bring that person back into your focus is the thing to do.

Wrapped up in life

Instead of being wrapped tightly in the thoughts of your job or going to the gym after work, how about cooking a special meal for someone or bringing a small gift of flowers on your way home? Wrap yourself out of your internal self-thoughts of what you need right now and bring your thoughts back to wrapping yourself in the person you love. Life is fragile and needs soft thoughts filled with smiles, love and hope.

10. Mindful living

Be still and hear the voices of your inner being telling you how important taking care of yourself is. You must be a light onto yourself in order to be a service to others. Find kind ways to center yourself in stillness and warmth. Allow your soul to be your guide; showing you the way toward wellness in mind, body and soul. Be mindful of where you are in life without the distractions of daily events that move you toward disharmony. Your light becomes an energy that can be passed along to others when you are well and focused.

Body

Take care of your body today with some slow moving exercises that allow you to create your own dance.

Mind

Find challenges with your mind that allow you to think deeper than usual; there you will be creative and in touch.

Soul

Plan some soulful ways that deepen your internal spirit; allowing you to touch your *heart center*; brining some joy to others. Soulful and kind ways that touch others in meaningful and healing ways will come back to you.

11. China Doll

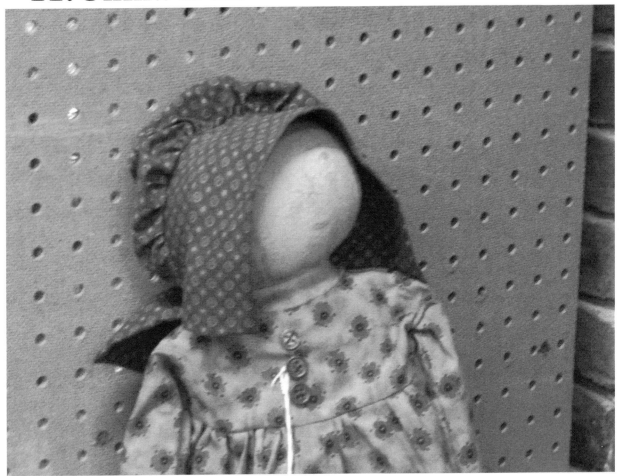

Dolls are important for the playtime in your life

Sometimes I feel like a fragile China Doll that has been broken too many times. And then I think about my soft, cuddly dolls that I can hold on tightly to. When my granddaughter asked to play with a China doll I told her, "Play is much more fun with something you can cuddle." She agreed and cuddled her soft, warm doll.

When I was young I thought that others had to help me put the pieces of life together but now I am stronger; realizing that only I can find the missing pieces and put myself together. Now I don't break much because my internal soul guides me toward knowing that things are made to be broken and if we are strong, centered and relentless, things come together with the pieces falling in place. And when there is a missing piece to your puzzle it is alright to go on without that piece because all the other pieces are special too. I told my granddaughter about missing pieces recently, "It does not matter that the picture puzzle of *Ariel the Mermaid* does not have all the pieces, you can still see her beauty even with some things missing."

12. Hang in there

Even when you are not feeling hopeful and excited about life's adventures, you need to hang in there and do some meaningful things in life.

Doing

What brings upon the things that you need and want in life is doing. Hold on to some *doing things* in life. Do for others who may benefit from your help, do for yourself some special things that make you smile because actions really do speak louder than words.

Remember when?

Your actions are what others remember the most about you. They remember when you picked them up after an accident they had or when you gave them 50 dollars and said, "Do not think about returning the money because it is a gift at a needed time." Or the time you lent your car to someone when their car was in the shop, or taking someone to a doctor's appointment when they needed a ride and someone to be with them for the good or bad news. So hang in there helping others because it truly helps you to feel better about yourself and the good things you do.

13. Togetherness

Looking and touching some old things can bring about connection

Find a way today to be connected to the person you love whether it is a tiny kiss on the cheek or a hug this morning; whatever it is that you do connects your souls. The term soul mate is not just a person who comes into your life all full of love and togetherness.

Soul mates take years of development; encouraging each other through the years, talking things out when there is a problem, and loving unconditionally. Move on together with your loved one; allowing for some mistakes to be made; we are all human. Do everything you can to nourish your partnership and apologize immediately when you know you are wrong, and even when you do not feel you are wrong because everyone has their own perspective in life's steps toward the open door. The last open door will have the light of angels waiting for you with your flaws, bad and good memories and the many thoughtful things you did with your partner to bring on togetherness.

14. Moving forward

Always move forward never looking back at the things that you may feel are mistakes or unfortunate happenings. Every single moment in life has value. The present moment is all that you have so savor it now and make it meaningful and beautiful. Love deeply, even if it brings you grief and sadness. Love is all that there really is in life so value it with all you have inside your soul.

People will move in and out of your life. You do not have control over who is gone or stays. Be solid and strong with the ones who stay and help you move toward wellness in mind, body and spirit. Be like a tree with strong branches that stretch to the sky; hovering and protecting others as you look down seeing the entire picture, and work hard on your strength and flexibility; knowing that you have to bend in order to make things right in life.

Be the one who apologizes first; telling the other person that you will try harder to make things better for both of you. Let it be okay to make mistakes because mistakes teach you lessons that you would not have learned very well if you did not try over and over again.

15. My kindness to you

When all you see is the abstract, be patient and you will see the beauty

I know you have pain inside that you cannot seem to deal with. And this pain has been passed onto me so that I have to do something with it. At first I thought I should be just like you and become angry about my pain. Then I tried stuffing it down into my soul so that it does not appear as anger anymore, but a lot of sadness started coming to the surface, telling me that my job was not done well, and I had to do something else with the pain.

And then my soul woke up wondering why I kept stuffing things down into my heart center and it gave me a nudge saying, " You have to do something else with this grief because it is becoming overwhelming and I will not be able to hold on to healing ways for you. You will become sick if you continue on this path." Just when I felt like giving up, a thought came to me of what I had to do. It was so simple. All I have to do is to continue showing you kindness and loving you unconditionally. Only then would the pain slowly move away from both of us.

16. Patient ways

I truly want to be more patient than I am right now.

And in the practice of patience I have come to believe that it is one of the hardest lessons for me. I want... I need... I got to... Please give me... all *self-words* that tending. These wants and needs have to simmer down so that I can focus on my new ability to develop patience in a disciplined way; knowing that things will come as they are supposed to without pushing too hard.

To me, waiting is like watching paint dry; you touch it, and it is still sticky. And then you look at where you touched it, and you have to paint it over again because you messed it up! If you would have left it alone, there would have been much less work. Sometimes relationships are like that too. You have to allow you and your partner to develop some loving ways. In the beginning of romantic love it is easy to be patient; you are star struck and in love. But when the romantic ways simmer down, you have to slowly add some zest to your lives; showing each other that you care in different ways and it may not be easy to keep the flame growing, but you can with some patience.

Do not push

And when you push too hard, you pay the consequences of stressful feelings and thoughts. You may feel down about why you cannot just get what you need, causing much drama in your life that is not good; causing much anxiety. Stressful waiting, tapping your foot and talking about what you need right now is not going to get you anywhere. Try moving along your path without the drama and stressful times by practicing being patient.

Discipline and patience are your guides

You can discipline yourself on being more patient, but you have to take it one day at a time; hoping that your new found discipline guides you toward not only a patient way but providing a healing energy that you develop when you are patient with yourself and others.

17. Embrace

Stand strong pushing tightly against each other; back to back

The hug

Sometimes we forget that our *physical self* can help us with *emotional and spiritual selves.*

There is much study on the physical embrace of a hug and how it can not only settle you down emotionally but helps bring down blood pressure, and bring on a smile. When people hug, smile and laugh other low mood states such as sadness and grief simmer down. Rise today, embrace yourself physically; giving yourself a hug and then pass it along to someone you love. They will feel you in your hug, all the way down to their toes.

Embracing life in a meditative way

Calm your mind today with some meditation; embracing the stillness of your body and breath. Close your eyes and just be in the moment; caressing your mind, body and soul.

Soulful adventures

Find a place in a vision today. That place you like to go to with a blue sky, warm sand under your toes and clean fresh air as you ride along on a row boat rocking back and forth softly touching the warm water with your fingertips.

18. Mystical

Life is a mystical, glimmering miracle

Life shines like the stars in the sky, sending your sprinkles of light, and you can see the golds, shiny whites and shades of blues when you gaze above. Keeping your eye on your star, keeping you head straight, shoulders back and a hop in your step to get you through the day. Even in the bad times, there is always a glimmer of sunlight in the clouds just for you. Force a smile right now, but let the tears flow whenever you want them to; tears show you where the clarity is.

Swing

You can swing back and forth like a pendulum; slowing down, speeding up but always moving toward your passions. I find life is a mystical pathway filled with many happening; some good and some not so good. Do not let the bad times cloud your good times. Stay as centered as you can; keeping your posture straight as an arrow with shoulders back as you walk down you path in life. Do not fear what is about to happen to you because even if this moment is not the way you would like it to be, there will be many more moments filled with joy and happiness.

19. Get up just one more time

Climb up your ladder in life, getting up just one more time and begin again

Every time I stumble, I get up again, brush myself off and try again. That has been my *mode of operation* for most of my life. And because of it, not only do I never quit, I keep my life full of challenges. We do need challenges in life to *shake things up*; stirring the pot just one more time to prevent the soup from burning. Just like the soup, you have to do things that help the momentum in life's adventures.

Doing

It is not what you say each day that helps you to feel good about yourself; it is what you do each day. Today I plan on doing some good deeds that will help the person who I care about the most; someone dear to my heart that is struggling through life but like me, keeps getting up one more time. Sometimes it seems like a challenge, and sometimes it feels like a pleasant experience when I hand someone a cup of hot coffee who is outdoors working hard. Can you do something for someone today that will make a difference?

20. Pass on a miracle today

I believe in miracles. The miracle of birth and the miracle of sudden healing of someone who had been ill for a long are examples of miracles. Now the person is well, and doctors cannot figure it out. The cancer is gone, you are in remission. Those words are what everyone who finds out about their illness hopes to hear. Had the person wished themselves well? Is there power in being optimistic about your prognosis?

Maybe it is others who prayed for your recovery. There is much literature on the power of healing energy that can be sent to faraway places. You can send healing and prayers to others through meditative ways. Whatever happens, it can become a miracle because you can change your attitude about things; bringing about acceptance, gratitude and love. And when you love and accept whatever comes your way, life is better. Even if you have an illness that does not go away, your attitude about your wellness can help you to feel better.

Other miracles in relationships

Change can happen. Changing yourself is a miracle. You become that person you always wanted to be. You knew all along what you needed to do, and now you are doing it. You are more helpful, kind and loving to others now. You put others first; they are your priority instead of you. You become the change you want to see in others, and now they are following you; making the changes they need to make in order for you to have a harmonious life together. Pass on a miracle today by being a mentor to others.

21.Care

Allow people in to your soul; you know that place deep down inside

If you are a caring person you need to take time for yourself right now.

Caring people touch our lives every day physically, emotionally and spiritually. You know how much you care by the number of friends you have. People seem to gather around those who have loving touches in mind, body and spirit. If you are one of those people, I am here to tell you to care for yourself too. It is time; time to look at your needs; nourishing yourself so that you can continue helping others.

Find a place to just be. It can be a physical place like a park that you love to go to. Be there alone; allowing your spirit to guide you on what you need today. And then do it; do things that are just for you so that you can then fill yourself with the energy that you need to continue helping others. Replenish your soul, fill you mind with peaceful thoughts and special and positive words.

22.Every time you stumble

Keeping yourself in the center

It seems to me that every time I have a mishap, something good comes from it. Even when you think you are at rock bottom, you come up again, knowing that those lessons learned well will not be repeated. We learn by practicing things over and over again until we get them right. Do not get too down when you feel like life has given you one more challenge than everyone else.

First of all, it is not true; life gives us all the ups and downs. That is why there is so much literature on the *yin and yang* of things. Find your balance today, even if it is among some challenges. You need both the good and the bad to keep you in the center.

23.Change

Make the changes you need to make, even if they look different to others

Life is full of changes, some good and some not so good. I remember as a child, sitting on the edge of a cliff near the beach. I loved to sit there and just rock my feet back and forth, not thinking about anything in particular, just watching the waves come into shore as they pushed their way back and forth. This sitting brought me much comfort while growing up, and I would return there periodically as an adult to see if it still helped. And yes, the rising and falling of the blue waves with white tips, the smell of the lake and its crisp and clean air still helps me to stay centered in mind, body and spirit.

There have been many changes in my life since childhood, adulthood and now old age. Now I am stronger than I ever thought possible, and internally I can bring up that memory of the waves and the scent of freshness in my mind's eye any time I need a *tweak of wellness* in my life. Embrace change but use some of your past centering moments to find comfort and peace when you need to. Live your life knowing that there will always be something changing that you may or may not want or need. Change just is.

24. Waiting is difficult but sometimes you have to

Being patient is not something that I can do easily. I always feel the need to push things to the limit thinking that perhaps whatever it is that I want will come sooner if I give it a nudge. But that is probably the worst thing I could do if I truly want something to change in life. Change is slow, just like a drop of water dripping from the faucet; you can almost see it stretching its very long drop until it reaches the bottom of the sink, forever gone but not forgotten, especially if it is making a dripping sound in the middle of the night.

Where are you in the waiting game?

Are you a patient soul who has practiced many years to become an expert on the importance of discipline? *Good things come to those who wait* is a perfect saying for many of us. While you wait patiently for the next drop from the faucet, or you wait for that feeling of wellness after you take a brisk walk; waiting patiently is the key to your mind, body and spiritual growth.

25. Honest Times

Be an open book with many pages so that others know you inside and out

I would love to believe that I am an honest person but there are things that I hold deep down in my heart that I have never spoken to anyone and times in life that I would rather forget than remember. We all have them, and sometimes it helps to get it all out in the open; especially with relationships that are meaningful to you.

You may have someone in your life that deserves some disclosure of information that you have tucked into your *mind's eye*; that place where even you have limited recognition as to how many of the not so good things in your life evolved, took a life of their own and then ended.

Everything has a beginning, middle and ending, even relationships.

You have to work hard on yourself your entire life to make your personal being good, not just for others but for yourself too. Self- honesty is like self- confidence; you have to build it your entire life to be in tuned and rhythmic. So tuck away some of those memories, and disclose the ones that you feel may help you and others gain a better perspective of you and life as it unfolded. Then allow the present to be your guide to your future loving moments; creating new memories that feel good and balanced.

26. Hopeful Life

Life can become a hopeful event every single day when you travel down your path embracing all of your wonders. There is reason to believe that we all can stand strong, flexible and hopeful when we focus on what we have in life. Even when you are at your weakest moment, a hopeful thought comes into your mind and you smile thinking about what in life at this moment is keeping you strong.

Forgiveness is the first emotional state that I think about when I need strength in my life. Many people get through life, forgiving others but they never forgive themselves. If this is you; forgive yourself right now in this moment.

Abundance

Another area of strength for me is remembering how abundant my present life is; full of wonder and amazement. And when you start believing in yourself with the added confidence you have attained because you have forgiven yourself, things become even more abundant than you thought possible. You walk straighter, head held high with your shoulders back. You are flexible in mind, body and spirit, and people are beginning to notice the difference in you.

Enlightenment

The highest level of attainment in life is enlightenment; that place where your heart center meets your spirit and you sour above with visions of love, caring and hopeful moments, one after another. This wonder amazes you because you cannot believe that you have waited so long to become strong with abundance, flexibility and enlightenment.

And that tap you felt on your left shoulder the moment that you had this *ah-hah* moment is spirit telling you to keep on moving toward the wonder of living life well.

Feeling that spirit is telling you something?

27. Wisdom

The older I get, the wiser I am about everything.

In my 20's I used to fret a lot about many things I had no control over. Over and over again I thought what I really needed was happiness, and I struggled to find it, never realizing that it was inside of me and no one else could help me with being happier except for me.

In my 30's I became obsessed with thinking that I had to succeed at work; moving up the ladder and making something of myself; that too did not work out well. I was disappointed in most of my work; finding pleasure in things outside of work such as holistic modalities; finding yoga and stress reduction as the only way to calm myself down before, during and after work.

In my 40's many things changed including my perspective on life. I finished all the degrees I wanted to complete and finished another relationship. One after another it seemed but next time it would get better for me, I thought; maybe not!

In my 50's I found myself; the place where finding peace and harmony in my life became my passion; wishing that I had become calmer and more centered many years before.

In my 60's I have found that my wisdom has brought me to a balanced center. Now I watch others who are disappointed with life, and as an observer, I look on and give advice when asked on how to gain wisdom. Don't wait too long to be at your center. Wherever you are right now, stop and think of ways you can reach a softer, kinder, more centered self so that you do not have to wait until wisdom finally catches up to you.

Hoping that musing ways can help you to gain strength, balance and discipline in your life.

Doris

Made in the USA
Middletown, DE
14 February 2023

24049325R00020